The Cheese Lover's Cookbook: 50 Recipes

By: Kelly Johnson

Table of Contents

- Classic Mac and Cheese
- Cheese Fondue
- Baked Brie with Honey and Almonds
- Grilled Cheese Sandwich
- Cheese Stuffed Mushrooms
- Cheddar and Bacon Biscuits
- Spinach and Cheese Stuffed Chicken
- Four-Cheese Pizza
- Cheese and Herb Croissants
- Fettuccine Alfredo with Parmesan
- Cheese Quesadillas
- Cheese Soufflé
- Ricotta and Spinach Stuffed Shells
- Mozzarella Sticks
- Brie and Fig Jam Tart
- Cheddar and Ale Soup
- Goat Cheese and Beet Salad
- Cheese and Chive Scones
- Roasted Cauliflower with Parmesan
- Grilled Cheese with Tomato Soup
- Mac and Cheese Bites
- Stuffed Bell Peppers with Cheese
- Cheesy Garlic Bread
- Blue Cheese and Pear Salad
- Gratin Dauphinois
- Cheddar Bacon Deviled Eggs
- Cheese Ravioli with Pesto
- Cheese and Charcuterie Board
- Goat Cheese Stuffed Chicken
- Creamy Cheese Dip
- Baked Ziti with Ricotta and Mozzarella
- Cheese and Onion Frittata
- Stuffed Potatoes with Cheddar and Sour Cream
- Spinach Artichoke Dip
- Cheddar Cheese Waffles

- Gruyère and Mushroom Quiche
- Cheesy Broccoli Casserole
- Roasted Sweet Potatoes with Feta
- Pepper Jack Macaroni Salad
- Cheese and Sausage Stuffed Pastry
- Baked Cheddar Jalapeño Poppers
- Mushroom and Swiss Burger
- Feta and Cucumber Salad
- Cheese and Herb Pizza Rolls
- Ricotta Cheesecake
- Cheddar Cheese Soup
- Bacon-Wrapped Cheese-Stuffed Dates
- Creamy Goat Cheese and Garlic Pasta
- Mozzarella and Tomato Caprese Salad
- Caramelized Onion and Gruyère Tart

Classic Mac and Cheese

Ingredients

- 8 oz elbow macaroni
- 2 cups shredded sharp cheddar cheese
- 1 cup shredded mozzarella cheese
- 2 cups whole milk
- 2 tablespoons unsalted butter
- 2 tablespoons all-purpose flour
- 1 teaspoon Dijon mustard
- Salt and pepper to taste

Instructions

1. Cook the macaroni according to package instructions. Drain and set aside.
2. In a large saucepan, melt butter over medium heat. Stir in flour and cook for 1-2 minutes until golden.
3. Gradually whisk in milk, cooking until the mixture thickens.
4. Stir in the cheddar cheese, mozzarella, mustard, salt, and pepper.
5. Combine the sauce with the cooked macaroni. Mix well and serve hot.

Cheese Fondue

Ingredients

- 8 oz Gruyère cheese, shredded
- 8 oz Emmental cheese, shredded
- 1 garlic clove, halved
- 1 cup dry white wine
- 1 tablespoon lemon juice
- 1 tablespoon cornstarch
- 2 tablespoons kirsch (cherry brandy)
- Freshly ground black pepper and nutmeg to taste
- French baguette, cubed, for dipping

Instructions

1. Rub the inside of a fondue pot with the garlic halves.
2. In a small bowl, toss the shredded cheese with cornstarch.
3. Heat the wine and lemon juice in the fondue pot over medium heat.
4. Gradually add the cheese, stirring constantly until melted and smooth.
5. Stir in kirsch, pepper, and nutmeg.
6. Serve with cubed bread for dipping.

Baked Brie with Honey and Almonds

Ingredients

- 1 round of brie cheese (8 oz)
- 2 tablespoons honey
- ¼ cup sliced almonds
- Fresh thyme for garnish (optional)

Instructions

1. Preheat the oven to 350°F (175°C).
2. Place the brie on a baking sheet lined with parchment paper.
3. Drizzle honey over the top of the brie and sprinkle with almonds.
4. Bake for 10-12 minutes, until the cheese is soft and the almonds are golden.
5. Garnish with fresh thyme and serve with crackers or sliced baguette.

Grilled Cheese Sandwich

Ingredients

- 4 slices of bread
- 4 tablespoons butter, softened
- 2 cups shredded cheddar cheese (or preferred cheese)

Instructions

1. Butter one side of each bread slice.
2. Heat a skillet over medium heat.
3. Place one slice of bread, butter side down, on the skillet. Add cheese, then top with another slice of bread, butter side up.
4. Grill until golden and crispy on both sides, about 3-4 minutes per side.
5. Remove from the skillet, slice, and serve hot.

Cheese Stuffed Mushrooms

Ingredients

- 12 large white mushrooms, stems removed
- 1/2 cup cream cheese, softened
- 1/2 cup shredded mozzarella cheese
- 1 tablespoon grated Parmesan cheese
- 1 clove garlic, minced
- Salt and pepper to taste
- Fresh parsley for garnish

Instructions

1. Preheat the oven to 375°F (190°C).
2. In a bowl, combine cream cheese, mozzarella, Parmesan, garlic, salt, and pepper.
3. Stuff the mushroom caps with the cheese mixture and place them on a baking sheet.
4. Bake for 15-20 minutes, until the mushrooms are tender and the cheese is bubbly.
5. Garnish with fresh parsley and serve warm.

Cheddar and Bacon Biscuits

Ingredients

- 2 cups all-purpose flour
- 1 tablespoon baking powder
- ½ teaspoon salt
- ½ teaspoon baking soda
- ½ cup unsalted butter, cold and cubed
- 1 cup shredded cheddar cheese
- ½ cup cooked bacon, crumbled
- ¾ cup buttermilk

Instructions

1. Preheat the oven to 425°F (220°C).
2. In a large bowl, mix flour, baking powder, salt, and baking soda.
3. Cut in the butter until the mixture resembles coarse crumbs.
4. Stir in cheese and bacon, then add buttermilk until just combined.
5. Drop spoonfuls of dough onto a baking sheet and bake for 12-15 minutes, until golden brown.

Spinach and Cheese Stuffed Chicken

Ingredients

- 4 boneless, skinless chicken breasts
- 1 cup fresh spinach, chopped
- ½ cup ricotta cheese
- ½ cup shredded mozzarella cheese
- 1 tablespoon olive oil
- Salt and pepper to taste

Instructions

1. Preheat the oven to 375°F (190°C).
2. In a bowl, combine spinach, ricotta, and mozzarella cheese.
3. Slice a pocket into the side of each chicken breast. Stuff the chicken with the spinach mixture.
4. Heat olive oil in a skillet over medium-high heat and brown the chicken on both sides.
5. Transfer the chicken to the oven and bake for 20-25 minutes, until the chicken is cooked through.

Four-Cheese Pizza

Ingredients

- 1 pizza dough (store-bought or homemade)
- 1/2 cup marinara sauce
- ½ cup shredded mozzarella cheese
- ½ cup crumbled goat cheese
- ¼ cup grated Parmesan cheese
- ¼ cup ricotta cheese

Instructions

1. Preheat the oven to 475°F (245°C).
2. Roll out the pizza dough on a floured surface and place it on a baking sheet.
3. Spread marinara sauce evenly over the dough.
4. Sprinkle all four cheeses over the sauce.
5. Bake for 12-15 minutes, until the crust is golden and the cheese is bubbly.

Cheese and Herb Croissants

Ingredients

- 1 package refrigerated croissant dough
- ½ cup shredded Swiss cheese
- 2 tablespoons fresh herbs (parsley, thyme, or chives)

Instructions

1. Preheat the oven according to the package directions.
2. Unroll the croissant dough and place a small amount of cheese and herbs on each triangle.
3. Roll up the croissants and place them on a baking sheet.
4. Bake according to package instructions, usually 12-15 minutes, until golden brown.

Fettuccine Alfredo with Parmesan

Ingredients

- 12 oz fettuccine pasta
- 2 tablespoons unsalted butter
- 1 cup heavy cream
- 1 cup grated Parmesan cheese
- Salt and pepper to taste

Instructions

1. Cook fettuccine according to package instructions. Drain, reserving some pasta water.
2. In a large saucepan, melt butter over medium heat. Add cream and simmer for 2-3 minutes.
3. Stir in Parmesan cheese, salt, and pepper, and cook until the sauce thickens.
4. Toss the cooked pasta in the sauce, adding pasta water to reach desired consistency.
5. Serve with extra Parmesan and fresh herbs if desired.

Cheese Quesadillas

Ingredients

- 4 flour tortillas
- 2 cups shredded cheddar cheese
- 2 tablespoons butter
- Salsa and sour cream for serving

Instructions

1. Heat a skillet over medium heat and melt 1 tablespoon of butter.
2. Place one tortilla in the skillet and sprinkle with cheese. Top with another tortilla.
3. Cook until the bottom is golden and the cheese starts to melt, about 2-3 minutes. Flip and cook the other side until golden and crispy.
4. Remove from the skillet, cut into wedges, and serve with salsa and sour cream.

Cheese Soufflé

Ingredients

- 2 tablespoons unsalted butter
- 2 tablespoons all-purpose flour
- 1 cup whole milk
- 1 ½ cups grated Gruyère cheese
- 4 large eggs, separated
- Salt and freshly ground black pepper

Instructions

1. Preheat the oven to 375°F (190°C) and butter a soufflé dish.
2. Melt butter in a saucepan over medium heat. Stir in flour and cook for 1-2 minutes. Gradually whisk in milk and cook until thickened.
3. Remove from heat and stir in cheese, egg yolks, salt, and pepper.
4. Whisk egg whites until stiff peaks form, then gently fold them into the cheese mixture.
5. Pour into the soufflé dish and bake for 25-30 minutes, until golden and puffed.

Ricotta and Spinach Stuffed Shells

Ingredients

- 12 large pasta shells
- 1 cup ricotta cheese
- 1 cup cooked spinach, squeezed dry
- 1 egg, beaten
- 1 ½ cups marinara sauce
- 1 ½ cups shredded mozzarella cheese
- Fresh basil for garnish

Instructions

1. Preheat the oven to 350°F (175°C).
2. Cook pasta shells according to package instructions, then drain.
3. In a bowl, combine ricotta, spinach, and egg. Stuff each shell with the ricotta mixture.
4. Spread marinara sauce in the bottom of a baking dish. Arrange the stuffed shells in the dish, then cover with mozzarella cheese.
5. Bake for 20-25 minutes, until bubbly and golden. Garnish with fresh basil before serving.

Mozzarella Sticks

Ingredients

- 12 mozzarella sticks, frozen
- 1 cup all-purpose flour
- 2 large eggs, beaten
- 1 ½ cups breadcrumbs
- ½ cup grated Parmesan cheese
- Vegetable oil for frying

Instructions

1. Heat oil in a deep fryer or large pot to 350°F (175°C).
2. Dredge each mozzarella stick in flour, dip in eggs, and coat with breadcrumbs mixed with Parmesan.
3. Fry in batches for 2-3 minutes, until golden and crispy.
4. Drain on paper towels and serve with marinara sauce.

Brie and Fig Jam Tart

Ingredients

- 1 sheet puff pastry
- 4 oz brie cheese, sliced
- 3 tablespoons fig jam
- Fresh thyme for garnish

Instructions

1. Preheat the oven to 375°F (190°C).
2. Roll out the puff pastry and place it on a baking sheet.
3. Spread fig jam over the center, leaving a border around the edges.
4. Arrange the brie slices on top of the jam.
5. Bake for 20-25 minutes, until the pastry is golden and puffed.
6. Garnish with fresh thyme and serve warm.

Cheddar and Ale Soup

Ingredients

- 2 tablespoons butter
- 1 medium onion, diced
- 1 carrot, diced
- 2 cups chicken or vegetable broth
- 2 cups milk
- 2 cups shredded sharp cheddar cheese
- 1 cup beer (ale)
- Salt and pepper to taste

Instructions

1. Melt butter in a large pot over medium heat. Add onion and carrot and sauté for 5-7 minutes until softened.
2. Add broth and bring to a simmer. Stir in milk and beer, and cook for 5 minutes.
3. Gradually add the cheddar cheese, stirring until melted.
4. Season with salt and pepper to taste.
5. Serve hot with crusty bread.

Goat Cheese and Beet Salad

Ingredients

- 4 cups mixed salad greens
- 2 roasted beets, sliced
- 4 oz goat cheese, crumbled
- ¼ cup toasted walnuts
- Balsamic vinaigrette for dressing

Instructions

1. Arrange salad greens on a platter.
2. Top with sliced beets, crumbled goat cheese, and toasted walnuts.
3. Drizzle with balsamic vinaigrette and serve immediately.

Cheese and Chive Scones

Ingredients

- 2 cups all-purpose flour
- 2 teaspoons baking powder
- ½ teaspoon salt
- ½ cup cold unsalted butter, cubed
- 1 cup shredded cheddar cheese
- 3 tablespoons chopped fresh chives
- 1 cup heavy cream

Instructions

1. Preheat the oven to 400°F (200°C).
2. In a bowl, combine flour, baking powder, and salt. Cut in butter until the mixture resembles coarse crumbs.
3. Stir in cheese and chives, then add cream. Mix until just combined.
4. Turn the dough out onto a floured surface and knead gently. Pat into a circle and cut into wedges.
5. Place on a baking sheet and bake for 12-15 minutes, until golden.

Roasted Cauliflower with Parmesan

Ingredients

- 1 head of cauliflower, cut into florets
- 2 tablespoons olive oil
- ½ cup grated Parmesan cheese
- Salt and pepper to taste
- Fresh parsley for garnish

Instructions

1. Preheat the oven to 400°F (200°C).
2. Toss cauliflower florets with olive oil, salt, and pepper.
3. Spread the cauliflower on a baking sheet and roast for 20-25 minutes, until golden.
4. Sprinkle with Parmesan and return to the oven for 5 more minutes, until the cheese is melted.
5. Garnish with fresh parsley and serve.

Grilled Cheese with Tomato Soup

Ingredients

- 4 slices of bread
- 2 cups shredded cheddar cheese
- 4 tablespoons butter
- 2 cups tomato soup (store-bought or homemade)

Instructions

1. Preheat a skillet over medium heat. Butter one side of each slice of bread.
2. Place cheese between two slices of bread, buttered side out. Grill in the skillet for 3-4 minutes per side, until golden and the cheese is melted.
3. Heat tomato soup in a pot over medium heat.
4. Serve the grilled cheese sandwich with a bowl of hot tomato soup.

Mac and Cheese Bites

Ingredients

- 2 cups cooked macaroni
- 1 ½ cups shredded cheddar cheese
- 1 cup breadcrumbs
- 1/2 cup milk
- 1 egg, beaten
- 1 tablespoon butter, melted
- Salt and pepper to taste
- Vegetable oil for frying

Instructions

1. Preheat the oven to 350°F (175°C) and grease a muffin tin.
2. In a bowl, combine cooked macaroni, cheddar cheese, breadcrumbs, milk, egg, butter, salt, and pepper.
3. Spoon the mixture into the muffin tin and press down to compact.
4. Bake for 15-20 minutes, until golden brown and crispy.
5. Let cool slightly before serving.

Stuffed Bell Peppers with Cheese

Ingredients

- 4 bell peppers, tops cut off and seeds removed
- 1 cup cooked rice
- 1 cup shredded cheddar cheese
- 1 cup cooked ground beef or turkey
- 1 can diced tomatoes
- 1 teaspoon Italian seasoning
- Salt and pepper to taste

Instructions

1. Preheat the oven to 375°F (190°C).
2. In a bowl, combine cooked rice, ground beef, tomatoes, Italian seasoning, salt, and pepper.
3. Stuff the bell peppers with the mixture, then top with shredded cheddar cheese.
4. Place the peppers in a baking dish and cover with foil.
5. Bake for 25-30 minutes, removing the foil for the last 10 minutes to melt the cheese.
6. Serve hot.

Cheesy Garlic Bread

Ingredients

- 1 loaf Italian bread
- 1/2 cup unsalted butter, softened
- 3 garlic cloves, minced
- 1 cup shredded mozzarella cheese
- 1/4 cup grated Parmesan cheese
- Fresh parsley, chopped

Instructions

1. Preheat the oven to 375°F (190°C).
2. Slice the bread into thick pieces.
3. Mix the butter and garlic together, then spread on each slice of bread.
4. Sprinkle with mozzarella and Parmesan cheese.
5. Bake for 10-12 minutes, until the cheese is melted and bubbly.
6. Garnish with fresh parsley and serve.

Blue Cheese and Pear Salad

Ingredients

- 4 cups mixed greens
- 2 pears, sliced
- 4 oz blue cheese, crumbled
- 1/4 cup candied pecans
- Balsamic vinaigrette dressing

Instructions

1. Arrange the mixed greens on a plate.
2. Top with pear slices, crumbled blue cheese, and candied pecans.
3. Drizzle with balsamic vinaigrette and serve immediately.

Gratin Dauphinois

Ingredients

- 4 large russet potatoes, thinly sliced
- 1 ½ cups heavy cream
- 1 cup grated Gruyère cheese
- 2 cloves garlic, minced
- Salt and pepper to taste

Instructions

1. Preheat the oven to 375°F (190°C).
2. Grease a baking dish and rub the inside with garlic.
3. Layer the potato slices in the dish, then pour the cream over the top.
4. Season with salt and pepper, then top with Gruyère cheese.
5. Cover with foil and bake for 45 minutes.
6. Remove the foil and bake for an additional 15-20 minutes, until golden and bubbly.

Cheddar Bacon Deviled Eggs

Ingredients

- 6 hard-boiled eggs, peeled and halved
- 1/4 cup mayonnaise
- 1/4 cup shredded cheddar cheese
- 2 tablespoons crumbled bacon
- 1 teaspoon Dijon mustard
- Salt and pepper to taste

Instructions

1. Remove the yolks from the boiled eggs and place them in a bowl.
2. Mash the yolks with mayonnaise, Dijon mustard, cheddar cheese, and bacon.
3. Season with salt and pepper, then spoon or pipe the mixture back into the egg whites.
4. Garnish with additional bacon and cheese, and serve chilled.

Cheese Ravioli with Pesto

Ingredients

- 1 package cheese ravioli (fresh or frozen)
- 1/4 cup pesto sauce
- 1 tablespoon olive oil
- Fresh Parmesan for garnish

Instructions

1. Cook the ravioli according to package instructions.
2. Drain and toss with olive oil and pesto sauce.
3. Serve topped with fresh Parmesan.

Cheese and Charcuterie Board

Ingredients

- Assorted cheeses (brie, cheddar, goat cheese, gouda)
- Assorted meats (salami, prosciutto, chorizo)
- Crackers, baguette slices, and nuts
- Fresh fruits (grapes, figs, apple slices)
- Honey and jam

Instructions

1. Arrange the cheeses, meats, crackers, and fruits on a large platter.
2. Add small bowls of honey and jam for dipping.
3. Serve as an appetizer or party dish.

Goat Cheese Stuffed Chicken

Ingredients

- 4 chicken breasts
- 4 oz goat cheese
- 2 tablespoons fresh basil, chopped
- Salt and pepper to taste
- 1 tablespoon olive oil

Instructions

1. Preheat the oven to 375°F (190°C).
2. Cut a pocket into each chicken breast and stuff with goat cheese and basil.
3. Season with salt and pepper, then secure with toothpicks.
4. Heat olive oil in a skillet over medium-high heat and sear the chicken for 3-4 minutes on each side.
5. Transfer to the oven and bake for 20-25 minutes, until the chicken is cooked through.

Creamy Cheese Dip

Ingredients

- 8 oz cream cheese, softened
- 1 cup shredded cheddar cheese
- 1/2 cup sour cream
- 1/4 cup milk
- 1 teaspoon garlic powder
- 1 teaspoon onion powder
- Salt and pepper to taste

Instructions

1. In a saucepan, combine all ingredients and heat over medium heat, stirring until the cheese melts and the mixture is smooth.
2. Serve with tortilla chips or vegetables for dipping.

Baked Ziti with Ricotta and Mozzarella

Ingredients

- 1 lb ziti pasta
- 2 cups marinara sauce
- 1 cup ricotta cheese
- 2 cups shredded mozzarella cheese
- 1/4 cup grated Parmesan cheese
- Fresh basil for garnish

Instructions

1. Preheat the oven to 375°F (190°C).
2. Cook the ziti according to package instructions, then drain.
3. In a bowl, mix the pasta with marinara sauce, ricotta, and half of the mozzarella cheese.
4. Transfer to a baking dish and top with the remaining mozzarella and Parmesan.
5. Bake for 20-25 minutes, until bubbly and golden.
6. Garnish with fresh basil before serving.

Cheese and Onion Frittata

Ingredients

- 6 large eggs
- 1 cup shredded cheddar cheese
- 1 medium onion, thinly sliced
- 1 tablespoon olive oil
- Salt and pepper to taste
- Fresh herbs (optional for garnish)

Instructions

1. Preheat the oven to 375°F (190°C).
2. Heat olive oil in an oven-safe skillet over medium heat.
3. Add the sliced onions and cook for 5-7 minutes until softened.
4. In a bowl, whisk the eggs with salt and pepper, then stir in the shredded cheese.
5. Pour the egg mixture over the onions in the skillet.
6. Cook for 3-4 minutes until the edges begin to set, then transfer the skillet to the oven.
7. Bake for 8-10 minutes or until the eggs are fully set.
8. Garnish with fresh herbs if desired, then slice and serve.

Stuffed Potatoes with Cheddar and Sour Cream

Ingredients

- 4 large russet potatoes
- 1 cup shredded cheddar cheese
- 1/2 cup sour cream
- 2 tablespoons butter
- 1/4 cup milk
- Salt and pepper to taste
- Chives or green onions, chopped (for garnish)

Instructions

1. Preheat the oven to 400°F (200°C).
2. Pierce the potatoes with a fork and bake for 45-50 minutes until tender.
3. Slice the potatoes in half lengthwise and scoop out the flesh into a bowl, leaving a small border.
4. Mash the potato flesh with butter, sour cream, milk, salt, and pepper.
5. Stir in half of the cheddar cheese, then spoon the mixture back into the potato skins.
6. Sprinkle with the remaining cheddar cheese and bake for an additional 10-15 minutes, until the cheese is melted and bubbly.
7. Garnish with chopped chives or green onions before serving.

Spinach Artichoke Dip

Ingredients

- 1 cup cooked spinach, drained and chopped
- 1 can (14 oz) artichoke hearts, drained and chopped
- 8 oz cream cheese, softened
- 1/2 cup mayonnaise
- 1/2 cup grated Parmesan cheese
- 1 cup shredded mozzarella cheese
- 1 teaspoon garlic powder
- Salt and pepper to taste

Instructions

1. Preheat the oven to 375°F (190°C).
2. In a mixing bowl, combine spinach, artichokes, cream cheese, mayonnaise, Parmesan, mozzarella, garlic powder, salt, and pepper.
3. Transfer the mixture to a greased baking dish and smooth the top.
4. Bake for 20-25 minutes, until golden and bubbly.
5. Serve warm with crackers, chips, or vegetables.

Cheddar Cheese Waffles

Ingredients

- 2 cups all-purpose flour
- 1 1/2 teaspoons baking powder
- 1/2 teaspoon salt
- 1/2 teaspoon garlic powder
- 2 large eggs
- 1 cup milk
- 1/2 cup melted butter
- 1 1/2 cups shredded cheddar cheese

Instructions

1. Preheat your waffle iron.
2. In a large bowl, combine flour, baking powder, salt, and garlic powder.
3. In a separate bowl, whisk together eggs, milk, and melted butter.
4. Pour the wet ingredients into the dry ingredients and mix until combined.
5. Fold in the shredded cheddar cheese.
6. Lightly grease the waffle iron and cook the waffles according to the manufacturer's instructions until golden brown.
7. Serve immediately with toppings of your choice, such as sour cream or salsa.

Gruyère and Mushroom Quiche

Ingredients

- 1 pie crust, pre-baked
- 1 cup shredded Gruyère cheese
- 1 cup mushrooms, sliced
- 1/2 cup heavy cream
- 3 large eggs
- 1/4 teaspoon nutmeg
- Salt and pepper to taste
- 1 tablespoon olive oil

Instructions

1. Preheat the oven to 375°F (190°C).
2. Heat olive oil in a skillet over medium heat.
3. Add the sliced mushrooms and sauté until softened, about 5 minutes.
4. In a mixing bowl, whisk together eggs, heavy cream, nutmeg, salt, and pepper.
5. Spread the sautéed mushrooms evenly over the pre-baked pie crust.
6. Pour the egg mixture over the mushrooms, then sprinkle with shredded Gruyère cheese.
7. Bake for 25-30 minutes, until the quiche is set and golden on top.
8. Let cool slightly before slicing and serving.

Cheesy Broccoli Casserole

Ingredients

- 4 cups broccoli florets, steamed
- 1 cup shredded cheddar cheese
- 1 can (10.5 oz) cream of mushroom soup
- 1/2 cup sour cream
- 1/4 cup milk
- 1/2 cup breadcrumbs
- 2 tablespoons butter, melted
- Salt and pepper to taste

Instructions

1. Preheat the oven to 375°F (190°C).
2. In a large bowl, mix steamed broccoli, cheddar cheese, cream of mushroom soup, sour cream, milk, salt, and pepper.
3. Transfer the mixture to a greased baking dish.
4. In a small bowl, mix breadcrumbs and melted butter, then sprinkle over the casserole.
5. Bake for 20-25 minutes, until the casserole is hot and bubbly, and the topping is golden brown.

Roasted Sweet Potatoes with Feta

Ingredients

- 4 medium sweet potatoes, peeled and cubed
- 1 tablespoon olive oil
- Salt and pepper to taste
- 1/2 cup crumbled feta cheese
- 2 tablespoons fresh parsley, chopped

Instructions

1. Preheat the oven to 400°F (200°C).
2. Toss the cubed sweet potatoes with olive oil, salt, and pepper.
3. Spread the sweet potatoes in a single layer on a baking sheet and roast for 25-30 minutes, until tender.
4. Remove from the oven and sprinkle with crumbled feta cheese.
5. Garnish with chopped parsley and serve warm.

Pepper Jack Macaroni Salad

Ingredients

- 2 cups elbow macaroni, cooked
- 1 cup shredded pepper jack cheese
- 1/2 cup mayonnaise
- 1 tablespoon Dijon mustard
- 1 tablespoon apple cider vinegar
- 1/2 red bell pepper, diced
- 1/2 cup chopped green onions
- Salt and pepper to taste

Instructions

1. In a large bowl, combine cooked macaroni, shredded pepper jack cheese, mayonnaise, Dijon mustard, vinegar, red bell pepper, and green onions.
2. Stir until well combined and season with salt and pepper.
3. Chill in the refrigerator for at least 1 hour before serving.

Cheese and Sausage Stuffed Pastry

Ingredients

- 1 package puff pastry, thawed
- 1/2 lb sausage, cooked and crumbled
- 1 cup shredded mozzarella cheese
- 1/4 cup grated Parmesan cheese
- 1/4 cup chopped green onions
- 1 egg, beaten

Instructions

1. Preheat the oven to 400°F (200°C).
2. Roll out the puff pastry on a lightly floured surface.
3. In a bowl, mix the cooked sausage, mozzarella, Parmesan, and green onions.
4. Place a spoonful of the sausage mixture in the center of each pastry square.
5. Fold the pastry over the filling and seal the edges.
6. Brush the tops with the beaten egg.
7. Bake for 15-20 minutes, until golden brown and puffed.
8. Serve warm.

Baked Cheddar Jalapeño Poppers

Ingredients

- 12 fresh jalapeños, halved and seeded
- 8 oz cream cheese, softened
- 1 cup shredded cheddar cheese
- 1/2 teaspoon garlic powder
- 1/4 teaspoon smoked paprika
- Salt and pepper to taste
- 1/2 cup breadcrumbs

Instructions

1. Preheat the oven to 375°F (190°C).
2. Slice the jalapeños in half lengthwise and remove the seeds.
3. In a bowl, mix cream cheese, shredded cheddar, garlic powder, smoked paprika, salt, and pepper until smooth.
4. Stuff each jalapeño half with the cheese mixture.
5. Sprinkle breadcrumbs on top of each stuffed jalapeño.
6. Place the jalapeños on a baking sheet lined with parchment paper and bake for 20-25 minutes, until golden and bubbly.
7. Serve hot as a spicy snack or appetizer.

Mushroom and Swiss Burger

Ingredients

- 1 lb ground beef
- 4 slices Swiss cheese
- 1 cup mushrooms, sliced
- 1 tablespoon butter
- 4 burger buns
- Salt and pepper to taste
- Lettuce, tomato, and pickles for garnish

Instructions

1. Form the ground beef into 4 burger patties and season with salt and pepper.
2. In a skillet, melt butter over medium heat.
3. Add the sliced mushrooms and cook for 5-7 minutes until softened and golden. Set aside.
4. Grill or pan-fry the burger patties to your desired doneness.
5. During the last minute of cooking, place a slice of Swiss cheese on each patty to melt.
6. Toast the burger buns in the skillet or on the grill.
7. Assemble the burgers by placing a patty on the bottom bun, followed by a spoonful of sautéed mushrooms.
8. Top with lettuce, tomato, pickles, and the top bun. Serve with fries or chips.

Feta and Cucumber Salad

Ingredients

- 1 cucumber, diced
- 1/2 cup crumbled feta cheese
- 1/4 red onion, thinly sliced
- 1 tablespoon olive oil
- 1 tablespoon red wine vinegar
- Salt and pepper to taste
- Fresh dill or parsley for garnish

Instructions

1. In a large bowl, combine the diced cucumber, crumbled feta, and red onion.
2. Drizzle with olive oil and red wine vinegar, then toss to combine.
3. Season with salt and pepper to taste.
4. Garnish with fresh dill or parsley before serving.
5. Serve chilled as a light side dish or appetizer.

Cheese and Herb Pizza Rolls

Ingredients

- 1 package pizza dough
- 1 cup shredded mozzarella cheese
- 1/2 cup grated Parmesan cheese
- 1 tablespoon dried oregano
- 1 tablespoon dried basil
- 1/4 teaspoon garlic powder
- 1 tablespoon olive oil

Instructions

1. Preheat the oven to 375°F (190°C).
2. Roll out the pizza dough into a rectangle on a lightly floured surface.
3. Sprinkle the mozzarella cheese, Parmesan cheese, oregano, basil, and garlic powder evenly over the dough.
4. Roll up the dough tightly, then slice into 1-inch pieces.
5. Arrange the pizza rolls on a baking sheet lined with parchment paper.
6. Brush the tops with olive oil.
7. Bake for 12-15 minutes, until the rolls are golden and the cheese is bubbly.
8. Serve warm as a savory snack or appetizer.

Ricotta Cheesecake

Ingredients

- 1 1/2 cups ricotta cheese
- 1 1/2 cups cream cheese, softened
- 1 cup sugar
- 1 teaspoon vanilla extract
- 3 large eggs
- 1/4 cup all-purpose flour
- 1/4 cup heavy cream
- 1/4 teaspoon salt

Instructions

1. Preheat the oven to 325°F (163°C).
2. In a large mixing bowl, beat together ricotta cheese, cream cheese, sugar, and vanilla until smooth.
3. Add the eggs one at a time, beating well after each addition.
4. Mix in the flour, heavy cream, and salt until combined.
5. Pour the batter into a greased 9-inch springform pan.
6. Bake for 55-60 minutes, until the cheesecake is set and lightly golden on top.
7. Let the cheesecake cool completely before removing from the pan and refrigerating for at least 4 hours.
8. Serve chilled, optionally topped with fresh berries or a fruit compote.

Cheddar Cheese Soup

Ingredients

- 4 tablespoons butter
- 1 small onion, finely chopped
- 2 cups vegetable or chicken broth
- 2 cups shredded cheddar cheese
- 1 cup milk
- 1/2 cup heavy cream
- 1/4 cup flour
- Salt and pepper to taste
- Fresh chives for garnish

Instructions

1. In a large pot, melt the butter over medium heat.
2. Add the chopped onion and sauté until soft, about 5 minutes.
3. Stir in the flour and cook for 1-2 minutes to form a roux.
4. Slowly whisk in the broth, followed by the milk and heavy cream.
5. Bring the soup to a simmer and cook for 10-12 minutes, until thickened.
6. Stir in the shredded cheddar cheese and cook until melted and smooth.
7. Season with salt and pepper to taste.
8. Serve hot, garnished with fresh chives.

Bacon-Wrapped Cheese-Stuffed Dates

Ingredients

- 12 large Medjool dates, pitted
- 4 oz goat cheese or cream cheese
- 6 slices bacon, cut in half
- Toothpicks for securing

Instructions

1. Preheat the oven to 375°F (190°C).
2. Stuff each date with a spoonful of goat cheese or cream cheese.
3. Wrap each stuffed date with a half slice of bacon and secure with a toothpick.
4. Place the bacon-wrapped dates on a baking sheet lined with parchment paper.
5. Bake for 15-20 minutes, until the bacon is crispy and golden.
6. Serve warm as a delicious appetizer or snack.

Creamy Goat Cheese and Garlic Pasta

Ingredients

- 8 oz pasta (such as spaghetti or fettuccine)
- 4 oz goat cheese
- 2 tablespoons olive oil
- 4 cloves garlic, minced
- 1/2 cup heavy cream
- Salt and pepper to taste
- Fresh basil for garnish

Instructions

1. Cook the pasta according to package instructions, then drain and set aside.
2. In a large skillet, heat olive oil over medium heat.
3. Add the minced garlic and sauté for 1-2 minutes, until fragrant.
4. Stir in the goat cheese and heavy cream, then cook for 3-4 minutes until the sauce is creamy and smooth.
5. Toss the cooked pasta into the sauce, stirring to coat evenly.
6. Season with salt and pepper to taste.
7. Serve garnished with fresh basil.

Mozzarella and Tomato Caprese Salad

Ingredients

- 2 large tomatoes, sliced
- 8 oz fresh mozzarella cheese, sliced
- Fresh basil leaves
- 2 tablespoons olive oil
- 1 tablespoon balsamic vinegar
- Salt and pepper to taste

Instructions

1. Arrange the tomato slices, mozzarella slices, and basil leaves on a plate.
2. Drizzle with olive oil and balsamic vinegar.
3. Season with salt and pepper.
4. Serve immediately as a refreshing appetizer or side dish.

Caramelized Onion and Gruyère Tart

Ingredients

- 1 sheet puff pastry, thawed
- 2 large onions, thinly sliced
- 1 tablespoon olive oil
- 1/2 teaspoon thyme leaves
- 1/2 cup grated Gruyère cheese
- Salt and pepper to taste

Instructions

1. Preheat the oven to 375°F (190°C).
2. Heat olive oil in a skillet over medium heat.
3. Add the sliced onions and cook for 20-25 minutes, stirring occasionally, until caramelized.
4. Stir in thyme, salt, and pepper, then remove from heat.
5. Roll out the puff pastry on a baking sheet and spread the caramelized onions evenly on top.
6. Sprinkle the grated Gruyère cheese over the onions.
7. Bake for 20-25 minutes, until the pastry is golden and the cheese is melted.
8. Slice and serve warm.

www.ingramcontent.com/pod-product-compliance
Lightning Source LLC
LaVergne TN
LVHW061957070526
838199LV00060B/4171